At the Brasserie Lipp

Michael Edwards taught at the universities of Warwick and Essex, before being elected Professor of Literary Creation in English at the Collège de France, Paris. Early volumes of poetry and critical works appeared in England; he then turned to French for further collections of poetry and numerous works on European literature, painting and music, on philosophy, language, and the Bible. The first Briton admitted to the Académie française, he has an Honorary Doctorate from the University of Cambridge, where he is also an Honorary Fellow of Christ's College. He has been awarded the OBE and a Knighthood in Britain, and the Légion d'Honneur in France.

Collections by Michael Edwards include

To Kindle the Starling
Where
The Ballad of Mobb Conroy
The Magic, Unquiet Body
Rivage mobile (Poems in English and French versions)
At the Root of Fire / À la racine du feu (Selected poems
with French translations by Anne Mounic)
In a Wide Bewilderment of Quiet

Other books include
Eliot / Language
Towards a Christian Poetics
Poetry and Possibility
Of Making Many Books
Raymond Mason

MICHAEL EDWARDS

At the Brasserie Lipp

CARCANET

First published in Great Britain in 2019 by
Carcanet Press Ltd
Alliance House, 30 Cross Street
Manchester M2 7AQ
www.carcanet.co.uk

A CIP catalogue record for this book is available from the British Library.
ISBN 978 1 784107031

The publisher acknowledges financial assistance from Arts Council England.

Typeset in England by XL Publishing Services, Exmouth
Printed and bound in England by SRP Ltd, Exeter

Contents

1

Sitting in Lipp's with this in-
fernal ticking in the ink I find myself
remembering the quiet of Manhattan, the low-slung
crooning cabs with Rolls-Royce engines
shushing the sidewalk buzz, gliding
on soft rubbers along the deep pile
of roadway like butlers in Wodehouse;
and did they really smell
so sweet? Was that Persian air
odours from the bay or whiffs of perfumed petrol?

*

In the church over there, which gave its name
to a whole way of life, and now squats
on a square devoted to the stars of the Fifties,
I heard all those years ago the handsome voice
of Pierre Emmanuel. Did I understand
the poems, with my Cambridge French? Were there truly
so many women, agog like Philaminte?
Poetry as fiery reason, he wrote, a mind
that has the good sense of a body wholly
in touch with the world and ready for the exact
exacting flames of the candid, the white-
hot depths. And then
the volume from the *T.L.S.* with his signature
shaking in the corner like an invalid
not long before dying, which by then had occurred.

*

A waiter, distrait, picks the wax from his ear.
The cars, with not a single Simca, go flying past,
honking like geese. I see
in the coffee grouts two boys on an empty road,
swinging their heels against a wall, waiting for the rare

prize of a motor-car, the brilliant
Triumph Gloria, swift-footed Lagonda,
ponderous Standard Vanguard,
to approach down the long perspectives
and enter their little books.

2

A hard rain splashes on the uneven centuries.
We were lucky whose childhood survived
the Second World War, though that is neither
here nor there when I recall the condemned
and crazy tenements down in the *treizième*
where painters of exotic speech perched in eyries
linked by filigree flights of stairs
and stop-gap corridors. They were the elders,
moiling all hours in this provisional world,
each in his cell, to prize
open the cryptogram, from zenith to abyss,
or conjure dazzling elsewheres with Prussian red
and yellow viridian. I felt foreign,
listening open-eyed as the talk passed round
with the budget cocoa, a heady brew.

★

That baby with the candid eyes squeezed by the sun
is probably the *me* the gods prefer
or dislike the least. I deal him
on the table, face up, a winner.
Installed on my mother's early-Norman shoulder,
he stares me out, smiling the way they do,
still-born in the country beyond recall,
on a shiny surface retruding memory.
Dammit, he's the me *I* prefer, touching her hair,
a chubby fellow, yet the little blighter,
innocuous in Shanklin in the summer of '39
and placed mostly naked on a Channel beach,
lifted his hands and feet promptly from the good sand
and registered dislike, so I was told.

★

Coffee on the Piazza Navona had followed
a station in Keats House, not that he ever
had one. The police
were busy already, stripping the walls,
burning the furniture, cursing their luck,
hurriedly fumigating the meagre room
of the little pig-sick foreigner, pains
his breathless body no longer needed. Beneath
a small pyramid he was being lowered
into the pasture, among the sheep and the goats.
With crowds in the circus scenting spring
and gushing waters plashing on marble basins
in the naked Roman light, one can mourn.

3

At Hastings, now, did we lose or win?
The English, underdogs then and *sympathiques*,
had slogged all down England from Stamford Bridge
(no, not from Chelsea; it's in the North)
and huddled, in the shield-ring, on a hill
by the hoar apple tree near Andredsweald.
You know the story: the dogged English
stood their ground, killing continued all day, until
the Normans made as if to make for their boats,
the cloth-capped English scampered after,
and were considerably hurt when the Normans turned and charged.
The natives took a drubbing, were plucked, and that was
one in the eye for English intelligence. One owes
allegiance to Harold as the rightful king
and thanks to William for most of history
and for having become, after so many stubborn Springs
and implacable Autumns, one of us.
As the sun hovers behind banking clouds,
Harold kneels among the tourists in the Waltham ruins.

★

I can imagine it, the Wehrmacht vaunting
in well-drilled high-kicking chorus lines
out there, along the stunned half-empty boulevard.
I can see the iron green that clads them
in the colours of myth and the Teutonic fir-forest,
and the Forties hair-dos of the girls that serve them
from behind bars in look-alike restaurants
in a thousand films; and I know
the decency of the two German lads
watching from a bridge as they smoked my father-in-law,
and his, caching arms in the wine-dark earth,
and walking away. England occupied,
insularity breached, one cannot picture.
But then, we won the war,

or we outlived it, as the man said,
through being entirely incapable of imagining
Hitler at Lords.

★

Whether the din that stunned the air
above a cornfield in the place of larks
was a demon patrol of Halifax or Lancaster,
the trace of that passing wonder in a six-year-old
survives in the warren of memory. Exning.
In the East, beyond Tashkent, and Samarkand.
Such a brief
translation to paradise (the scented orchard,
the open skies, the room, the conviction
of being elsewhere) from the Thirties estate
to which the child Sigismund usually belonged
visited my dreams for decades as a rare
vision. Though even the later
mile-high insect drone of perfectly civil
airliners traversing the garden heights
of our little house on the Heathrow flight-path
returns as the proper sound of gold-green summer.

4

Sitting here sipping at life it is easy
to float light-minded on the wavelets of now.
I remember, however, the terra firma
of the real world, which included, among other
things I might withdraw from the long and musty
sock of memory, debutantes and haystacks
coming out in their season, not that I made
much contact with either. Where are they now
(I mean it: where are they now?)
that time has pulled the staircase from under the ones
and parcels the others in glossy bin-liners?
After thirty, the real is history.
I think with bewildered affection of those
elders who passed their musing youth
wearing Oxford bags and surfing the crystal-set.

★

Puzzling over Wordsworth, I wonder how
he thought that he had seen the world's glory
vanish with childhood. Had he really
romped in Eden, or did he half-
create that memory in the murk of adolescence,
when he discovered the time of spots?
What I recall is a deal of wailing,
and gnashing of teeth, and of having been
a tyke of the first water. And yet
Vaughan, and his 'angel infancy'. Is it
a recurring dream, beamed from beyond
memory, or (grandfather Wordsworth,
I speak as a fool) a being unable
to be there for the future's brief and furtive
advents in corners caught unawares
by vivid, occasional, new-earthly light?

★

A world in my hand in the dark bedroom,
the glowing orange from the Christmas stocking
I see it now, was a toy Paradise,
a wonder to be remembered, and laid aside.
The sunlight accumulates in high windows
above the agreeable, city din,
as once the falling sunlight caught
haphazard, naturally, in the higher branches
of ash, and fir, and pine, like thrown
fires from the end of time, burning the unharmed
and chosen trees. The conflagration
insisted in the green and usual leaves,
consuming attention. I stood in the shadows
and swore with happiness, and watched like a quiet
maniac as the embers slowly faded,
and the bats burgeoned from the neighbouring barns.

5

Astaires curvetting through the evening throng,
bearing their trays like the Statue of Liberty
(with a glimpse of tango as they pass each other),
the domino waiters correct with each
shimmy of the hips and inerrant footwork
the rolling of the waves, as if the brasserie
were afloat, or all of us actors in
the restaurant scene of a Thirties motion
picture during the long days
of crossing the Atlantic. All of us were sick
on the Channel ferry with the 2CV suspension
and poor whaleroad-holding in the heaving straits,
until the white-uniformed and diocalm voice
of the Captain assured us all would be well
soon, as we passed 'under the lee of England'.
He was right, the unknown formula worked,
I saw the island and the island centuries
lean over the tiny boat to protect it.

*

Old swords, danged and kerfed,
unsmeared of blood in the slow-breathing
after-battles, these, heavy with age,
wieldy with use and cunning knowledge,
gleamed in the minds of the earliest English
as most of worth. Likewise words,
heard through mists on the open furze,
in the depths of shadowed woods, their warm
thunder rising from the dark body
to roll in the deliberately moving mouth
and part the double brattice of the teeth.
Old words in the ear, soundings of an earlier
speech and settlement in the world's things,
impress the here, the now. I find harbour,
a place for the soul, in seaboard, wharf and mooring.

It was a smooth though hardly adroit
Ambassador I drove down the Essex by-ways
and down through the flimsy, unresisting
cells of the centuries to the log church
Saxon adzes had cleft and pitched
in the thick of the wood as the wood's nub:
a house of trees to put their faith in.
Not the stare of a screech-owl but a rip of skin
from an icy Viking nailed to the door
greets, at the timber threshold, and outfaces
uncomprehending questions. Within,
my heart sank, gladly, in the undertow
of the old speech, as the ear's mind
heard in our many, unhurried steps
the naming and wedding tongue of the earth-bound,
sky-bound folk, speaking in ours.
'Floor', 'roof', 'opening', 'rightness', 'depth',
remind me of Greensted, a barn for words.
I stir the wood-ash in the cooling hearth
(here, in the champagne light of Paris)
and find the red fire, living still.

6

My answer to the eternal question is
in the kitchen of a house in Orsay to the south of Paris
(a town where Péguy had been and Mosley was),
at breakfast, I believe, it could have been lunch,
I think it was breakfast, we too were stunned.
And a year later it was Eliot's turn,
in the same small kitchen with the radio on,
the first of so many (radios, I mean,
though deaths as well). I'd always supposed
we'd meet, he'd talk, he'd like my poems,
and be the presence of the barbarous, uncanny
language that had entered and coolly opened
a mind unforewarned of such edges of being.
In the world that whirled indeed the real
was suddenly sly, indifferent, different,
and the work stepped back into the pages of history.

*

Drumming and clicking on the marble top
(tentative morse to any passing muse)
recalls the Eroica – the variations – the lucky
thirteenth and that sudden, stricken hand
falling with rhythmic jerks on the clinking
appoggiaturas, then skeltering by fits
down down the keyboard in zany close-up,
and under the soft round hat, Chico's grin.
Travelling the innerscapes of sound, Beethoven,
did you cross the frontier towards what may be
sidereal calms, or tundra with crystal cities
(strains of silence straining to be heard),
by clowning, cutting up ugly, tumbling
scherzando through disgrace notes into the unknown?

*

One can picture him walking by the water-furlongs,
conversing in the damp streets with civil neighbours,
examining with Hall the store of simples,
or making for London, his horse ambling
under him, through acres of rye, but not
not writing. The very idea! The mind
deserts one at his retiring, dismissing his genie,
at the cool detachment of the gentleman of Stratford.
We have
so much to learn from the man's indifference,
from playscripts in neglected corners of the playhouse,
from his knowledge of immortality, that it is nothing
on earth, from his sober practice of silence,
beyond poetry, his final period.

7

Did Racine discern the lacing of sweat
on the horse's neck, or hear the harness
creek and abrade, or feel the jar
of each hoof meeting the road as if
along his own four legs, while he galloped
ahead of the others to get the best room?
Now, as a sunburst hazes the window
and slopped wine drips from a neighbouring table,
a housefly whispers in my English ear
that it takes as much courage, when the moment comes,
energy and cunning, to forget all that
as to recall it, and make it matter.

*

Of being elsewhere in the one world,
as the same sun sheds an unfamiliar light,
or the mind journeys with the journeying moon,
I sing, sitting here, and remembering Exning.
We stepped from the train into fields of wheat,
into earthy, shoulder-deep, country lanes,
for the wide-eyed kid a vertiginous pastoral,
a paradise heightened by the passing warplanes'
jocund din. In a strange house,
a stranger to himself, he tasted the different
plums, marrows, radishes, he climbed
into the guardian thick of unknown trees,
and ran through the air
sparkling with the effusion of privet and honeysuckle.
That leap from danger (while the V2s crouched)
to another universe bordering Newmarket
returns unfelt, unthought of, whenever
I see things with another's eyes, moonshadows
people with ourselves a sleeping courtyard,
or a building in a shining window discards its usual look
and the sun sheds its familiar light.

By the village pond we encountered a black
Canadian pilot. A neat man,
I seem to remember, gentle of speech.
Back indoors, the boy in his book,
my mother was doomed for having been seen
talking to a darky. Though this was Methodism,
there was madness in it; yet who can judge
the errors of that innocent, guilty time?
Another day we rose as one and stepped
silent from the room, the black lid
having closed on the upright as the offended air
stiffened at the breathtaking title of the song
I'd suggested we join in among the hymns
we'd forgathered to intone in the Sunday parlour.
I was in disgrace, though ignorant of grace,
and pored in my mind over the marvellous lady
whose awaited coming would be round the mountains
when she came, whose pink pyjamas
regardless of weather, would emblazon the day,
whose wild, spectacular being was as more
than real as the manners of a coloured airman.

8

I recall my mother's name as a maiden
mostly for distant voices on the phone
checking for security. Dalliston. It's rare.
A variant of Dallinson, more audibly Englished.
A William D. came with the Conqueror,
or was here for Domesday, having left
lacy Alençon with a view to plunder
(it takes all sorts). 'Norman blood'?
Thinned for centuries by Anglian peasants
and over the border in Cambridgeshire,
neglected, unrecognised, voiceless, but then
why else this ludic and unseemly yen
for a foreign tongue, to hear it in the murmurs
of a known, unfamiliar world, and in
that friendly other who likes to take over,
moved by some blind, stubborn
stubborn gene
to travel the sounds of a kind of innocence?

★

The door swings to with a recurring *brlnk*.
A dog and a girl trot by on the trottoir.
Le Monde on a nearby table folds
a world of noise in a semblance of peace.
The cars prolong their mathematics, et là-haut
cette barbe à papa céleste qui s'effiloche.
(The gusts of wind on the Brighton front,
the eye-watering sun, the strangeness of adults.)
What do they know, these amiable aliens,
that they speak their minds, they pluck their words
from the world's tree regardless of Saussure,
and hear them glittering among the spoons, the glasses?
Dumb with amazement, I watch a fictive *neige*
fall on the dreamy outside, its coldness quite
close to the baffled silence of snow.

★

At Agincourt, the Duke of Alençon,
breached by a thrust quite possibly Norman,
fell supine on France, and in the clouding light
dipped his fingers in his guts and wrote
the sign of the bloody cross on his breast.
Did he? Did I make it up? Does it matter?
Poetry is a foreign language, way
down inside one, guilty as hell
like everything else, yet cannily innocent,
in league with things to say them as they are
or as they become in the resounding light.
The church over there sticks out like a sore thumb,
trees walk down the boulevard in search of the forest,
it would be fitting if the broken body
like the wounded soul bore the mark of pardon.

9

Paying guests in the temple of Aquae
Sulis Minervae, we walked alone
through labelled wonders, listening each,
in the visible silence, to the private voice
of the audio guide. Below the clean,
Jane Austen town, rain-soaked though made
for fine hues of changing sunlight,
the water was alive, green in the still
bath and sluicing in ruddy torrents
into conduits heady with steam. Do I look
through an inner window at the spring itself,
moving forever, breathing, here and there
seething with will? I stoop, and see
through the hot mist feeling the stone niches
dressed by the strength of Roman masons'
unknowing piety, primeval turf,
a patch of bitter-cold Britain where gods
appear and withdraw, shrouding themselves
in health-giving vapour.

*

Rupert, now: is it reasonable
to have been so furtively possessed,
in the quiet globe of recurring Christmas,
by a tailored boy-bear whose daily outings
made wonder familiar? The secrets of Nutwood
were an open book, its hills like Surrey's,
in the depths of the trees a pagoda, within
which a Chinaman more than real,
and Tiger Lily. Down spools of time,
far back in the reachable, improper self
where images began and the world became
visible, I seem to see
at the foot of the magic bed in the hours
before the day, the earnest of a gift

(sunlights on a field through a rusty gate),
the waiting present.

★

A rising ground, row before row
of boulders heaving the old earth
up to the air, where stone-black crows
and the sheen of light-winged gulls travel
the storming sky. The teeth of Carnac,
sown without haste, wait still
to draw one into the dragon, the earth-
monster who devours, with each step,
some petty fear, whole vanities of thought,
in its open mouth. As you climb through the force
of the sacred field, the orchard of rocks,
and lose all bearings but one, the ungodly stones
are slowly fewer and more and more huge.
They stand beyond understanding, they are
the dumb, merciless presence that calls
to this lowly, vertiginous height where one
is glad to be small in a wide bewilderment of quiet.

10

Villon through the café window: still
present in Paris, under the carnal
pomegranate, the piercing stars?
Make your stand, if you wish to know,
in the rue des Mauvais Garçons, and con
the priceless ballads of this lyrical bad lad.
Say over, where the sun still blinds the road
with blade-cold shadow, the things an ageing
delinquent knew, time and again,
by sinking up to his neck in truth:
wary pinch-bellied wolves, his pals,
forgiveness lurking in dangerous corners,
exact sins beating in the marrow
of the mind, conversion of the soul
in a turn of phrase, 'I am his',
and girls with bodies soft and smooth.
Can any good thing come out of gang-land?
Frenchie Villon, apache with a pen,
seated by freezing ink among
inveterate grudges, garret humours
(and every line a nice piece of work),
rehearses enough misdoings to ground
an angel, with more than enough unique
unsleeping honesty to bleach the devil.
Say what you like, he's not one of us;
he had the balls to let himself
be struck forever with perpetual clarity.

★

Hugged by the cold, curled in, and hooded,
so many strangers hurry on past,
their hands hidden, their eyes on the paving,
their shaggy breaths like wordless balloons.
We move such worlds, we brood like gods
on the small immensities we contain,

amenable galaxies, our own eccentric
earth, ceaselessly revolved, clung to.
What may not be
devised where desire and yielding forms
meet and court, by 'every man
in the dark, in the chambers of his imagery'?
Memory
swoons down the lift-shaft, pausing to invoke
shining phantoms, true and false,
futures of the self, avenues of the real.

★

Ghostly relentless kettledrums and trumpets
wounded his ear. From side to side
his locks flowed ('so soft, like a woman's,
my darling') as the neck-post twisted and jerked
to expel the noise, the devil's compulsive
self-same strain. Crossing
the bridges of the tragic town, passing
the sinuous Rathaus, or half-awake
in the window-alcove, he could not stop
the manic blare. Stricken Robert
Schumann (who perished the last, most wretched
of a stricken family) mastered at last
the ghastly theme, making that mockery
dance to his tune in perfect symphony.

11

Down our street slowly the hearse proceeds.
Accumulated behind, the traffic adopts its pace.
Of overtaking maybe the thought occurs,
but nobody fails to suppress it. The gleaming black
passes a few pedestrians whose respect
(for the dead, for death, for Charon's long
beribboned rare vehicle?) causes to stop,
my father removes his trilby, in his hand
his son's hand stiffens, at the unknown,
the intrusion of adult unease among
the sunlit houses. But that
was seventy years ago. Since then
everything has changed, bar the hidden fact.

★

The cold unfurls the breath of the still
heavy horse with shaggy ankles,
while the aproned milkman clunks a bottle
on the front step, and removes the empties.
The float ambles on to the next few houses,
revealing steaming droppings on the roadway.
The estate, mock-Tudor, overlies an orchard
whose trees are sleeping in endless back-gardens.
By the side road that leads to Ham Common and the Park,
a small farm surprises with its wondrous stenches.
Inside the man, the boy, his mind and senses
just as alert; inside the urban sprawl,
the earth and its creatures. (My father, not
given to deference, to Tory mummery,
uncovers his head.) In the centre of town,
in Kingston, in the Forties, a cattle market,
every Saturday, cows and pigs galore,
heedless of cinemas, shops and lorries,
a few miles from London, on a site called Fairfield.

★

What do you mean: what is real? Do you mean
to find the answer by speculation,
or questioning neurons, elementary particles?
In the secret earth, more-than-real primroses,
antirrhinums, golden rod
spoke their names and revealed their life.
And foxgloves on our neighbour's strange border. She would place
each year in my mother's hand some precious
lilies-of-the-valley, and I wondered
where was the valley, where the harmless dragons.
(The blue and white vertical stripes of his apron,
his rattling crate with the eight compartments.)
And the sweet, creamy, crinkly top-of-the-milk
mantling the cornflakes. These foolish things
remind me of you, an elsewhere here, a world
lost and, by your ghostly presence, becoming
the glimpse of something other. Childhood's light
burns one's conscience for having mislived,
one's ache for heaven now, and yet burns
now even brighter.

12

An urban world of long walks and milkbars
(later editions may require a footnote)
centred on certain evenings in the Kenya
Coffee House. Most English, with a hint
of African turbulence. What was the idea?
To be alone and out in the world, to write
poetry in a notebook to the smell of coffee,
and meet, maybe, friends or unknowns.
To be young is to be young without the thought
of being young. I must have looked up
as the moment ushered in a vision of glamour,
apparelled in white, impeccably polished,
and bearing a sophisticated poodle. She sat
facing me, names were exchanged, we were
worlds apart, I in my books,
she, it seemed, mainly in her looks,
until, unfailingly beside the point,
I mentioned Racine. 'I've an old edition',
she said, 'Would you like it?' Voiceless, I gazed.
The next week, the same apparition, the same
mannered poodle floated in,
bringing the said volume. It's quite rare.

*

The world of the Wurlitzer and suchlike wonders,
of the Saturday-morning flicks at the Regal and the shouting
'aloud with glee' of the kids gathered
to learn and merge their emotions at the larger-
than-their-life adventures of Kit Carsen and Roy Rogers,
was shattered one Sunday afternoon in the dark
of another cinema, Plato's cave.
Snug between my looming parents, I followed
hardly at all whatever it was
the uncanny adults were busy with
on their black-and-white wall, when out of the blue

a music from nowhere seized me and filled
all time and space. The opening salvoes
exploded inside me, I was all ear,
tempest-wrecked on infinite shores.
I'd like to pretend it was Lully, late Mozart,
who plucked me out; it was Tchaikovsky,
and into the bargain, the piano concerto.
But why not? That piece, under the supposed
film star fingers, happened to be the first
music to my ears, the rushing through
of another universe. I went home wondering
where was that music, and where was I?

★

'Kingston' meant 'shopping' to the boy in short trousers,
to be taken there by bus in his mother's hand.
The 65, if it matters, and it strangely does.
Everything, as taken for granted, had a name,
and the names were friendly ghosts, to be sounded,
listened to, doors, magic keys.
Smith's, that trained the tongue, was a hall
of silence, and wood, and sleeping books.
Lyons, black and white tiles, and a clue:
'tariff', on a board. And the cliffs, the infinite
world of Bentalls, with the moving staircases
('Bentalls') and people ascending and descending.
Yet that was the scenery, the ordinary wonder,
with Boots, and Woolworth's (now gone with the wind),
for, from an alley that descended long
and narrow to the river, as if intruding
from another universe issued the acrid
nose- and mind-glutting reek of a tannery.
It was potent! It met you as you passed
along the familiar, like a sword, an invitation,
the revelation of something lost or found.
Indecently real, pungent beyond belief.
His foot might have tried the shadowy ground
of the secret passage, have followed it, trembling

with anticipation, down to the swirling
quick waters. Memory cannot help
this ageing Bottom catch sight of that smell.

13

I assumed, Robert Lowell, you would interview me;
your absence was puzzling; I got the job.
On arrival at Essex I again looked forward
to our meeting, to years of acquaintance and speech,
only to learn that I'd not come to join
Caesar but to replace him. The air hung heavy and vexed
with poems that had found my ear and prevailed,
with your strong echo of Marlowe's mighty line.
You had left, and you returned once only, to read
in a warm growl some later poems,
seated, in command and hesitating
over certain words that gave you pause and pain
and that you thought aloud you might have to change.
You hurried away; we sank down in the lift,
with time only for polite, meaningless words,
or so it seemed. A brief confinement
in a small moving space, and not so much later
news of your death in a New York taxi.

*

Each line of the wholesome address (Charles
and Brenda Tomlinson) fills
my heart too full (Brook Cottage, as if
the English countryside, the country home
named your presence, and can it be
really, Ozleworth Bottom?) In a vale,
a depth, of dry-stone Gloucestershire, that laughing
signpost to origin, along the lane
inviting towards Eden: 'Not
suitable for motors'. Here, the snow
falls, is falling, with infinite gentleness, its flakes
wafting and rising as often as falling,
in Paris, in another world from yours,
another time, where so much time,
such distance of unfaithful intermittent memories

crossing the gulf, make one
stutter like this.

★

Early read, late met. At the Gare du Nord
you loomed from the unquiet smoke of the crowd,
your stirred greeting: 'It hasn't changed!'
elegiac eulogy of a steadfast station.
Your measured speech, Geoffrey Hill, your unmeasured
affability are cause of wonder, as,
in poem after poem, your fecund recalcitrance,
your wrestle with the crippling angel till the day broke.
Beauty, guilt, one rind: the English
language realises that; the English
language is just like us, is just,
or not, like us. Faced with an audience,
your lurking comedy, its sudden release
split sides. Great bear you had them
eating out of your paw. Who would have…?
Gruff, with timely grace. Paris is sad,
the brasserie dull in the after noon.
Geoffrey, where are you now? Lost
in the life that rounds our little sleep,
in wonder, untroubled praise.

Initially I was, and am,
M. E. my favourite subject (object), me.
The ME spread-eagled is guardian of the weal,
would you believe it? hoard-warden, watch-dragon
of hidden treasure. And
before and unwieldier to bear, the name
of that which is the question, not
Hamlet's, but who,
who is like God? I should
wear it as a tee-shirt, a phylactery
in every act, in each
elected word, yet those primal chums,
who shared the only world we knew, were not
wrong, and Eddy
(water stirring against the current, a small
turbulence) about
sums it up.

★

What's in a name? A jungle of high, soft
thorough-green summer fern enfolds the boy,
the child who fathered, as the poet said,
painfully me. Old English fern…
'ferne halwes', a far-off shrine.
Crouched among smells, thoughtful and knowing
nothing but closeness of soil and that here
the real earth is, the guarded secret,
his body wonders in the silent Park.
Slowly he stands in a globe of green light,
in a time not out of time but within.
Fern, he thought, each autumn became
bracken, its name when russet, dry,
crackling with brittleness. The new-found brake
burns on the hill. An afternoon
wintry sunlight in the mirrored café

ages me abruptly. Bracken, I know,
is simply the northern name, given
to ferns in all seasons. The Anglo-Saxons,
the Norsemen also speak today
in this common plant, *fearn* and *brakni*
shaping our mouths, our minds. But was he wrong
to believe in tender fern and in dark
breakable bracken? To assume a name
changes as light and presence change?

★

Listen to *bungalow*, wide-eared seven-year-old,
in the small front room contained in your small
measureless mind. And *verandah*, voiced
by an unsolved aunt, prickly with secret
and unseizable words. A queer
cupple apparently living in a low
bunga will tease your brain, until
a softly whirring verandah flying past
covers the sky in colours and waving giants.
Gardenshed is no less magic – listen!
cupboard, *doorway*, *passage*, all
vibrating with what they name, speaking
from the strange warm beings to which they lead.
In the murmurs and clinks of the café I remember
shadows processing on Seine-side façades
like smoke amid the evening lights thrown up
by the cool aquarium of a bateau-mouche.

Sitting. It's what poets do. They used to walk.
Over on the other bank, a youthful Baudelaire
'stumbled on words' while roaming the suburbs,
found a hint of rhyme 'at every street corner',
and 'hit upon whole lines' suddenly there.
Out in the country, Boileau would meet
the elusive word 'at a bend in the wood'.
Oh to scare workmen like Racine half-singing
tirades from *Mithridates* as they came into his head
pacing about the Tuileries building site!
Or terrify peasants at their task in Westmorland
with the booming voice of Wordsworth striding the hills!
But alas, we need our Moleskins or the backs
of envelopes, or else we settle down
on the fleshy parts with pen and pad.
The result is flabbiness about the middle
where the waist should be and, maybe, where
the rhythm should be taut with the future within it.
Happily the mind and a still body
are full to bursting with kinetic energy.

★

Drunk with caffeine, my heart beats
wildly with Bill Haley at this morning séance
as I watch the table rise, wobble and knock.
Typtology? It's Greek to me, but then always what
turns up, as I believe I said
at the Brighton conference, is unexpected, foreign
to planned. Lino on the floor, on the walls distemper,
but our back garden, now, its climbable trees,
and undergrowth, its smells
of lilac and pear, its promise that gave
with hardly an effort, onto
the jungle freedom of Ham Common and then
through a narrow gateway the continent of Richmond Park.

Africa in particular, but also Asia,
Australia, and both Americas at the end
of the endless garden. Not history, but one's own
story repeats itself, until the dulled brain
begins to twig. Court after court
in a Cambridge College, lead you on and
invite you in; open and close
and again open, showing you the way
of the world. At Hidcote the orchard,
whose parallel lines afford a mindly
exuberance to accompany the fruit abounding
in shady foliage, barely remains
in memory as you lose yourself in looking
at world upon world in the ceaselessly changing
improbable gardens to be discerned
through archways in hedges that entice you further
and farther in and beyond. Over the river,
the Hôtel de Sully has a first court crowded and small;
you walk through the screens to a second,
to a larger sky and the scent of box;
in a secret far corner a passage gives
entry to the Forest of Arden, known
locally as the place des Vosges. The coffee
is wearing off, but I have time to note
the statue of St. James popped out of the top
of his famous Tower like a champagne cork.

*

Seated, I walk
athletically in the mind, foot following foot,
not pounding the beat but
hearing in forward motion the stresses and strains
of rhythmic, mouth-animating music that only
the genie of the English language delivers: provided
you find the lamp, and rub the right way.
The neat ballet
of waiters with impeccable technique continues
all around me as, with lowered head,

I write what comes along the lane of the line,
following my nosy Parker. It must be
deadly serious and vitally comic,
open to the uncanny, unfinished present,
redeeming fear, and time, and laughter.
Crowds in the street
move this way and that, as if
a god with a stick
had disturbed the peace. The pity is real,
the image unoriginal, one needs
to contrive in the language keener eyes
for seeing the unconsciousness of death,
the ignorance of life. 'Quelle heure est-il?'
Today is holy
Saturday as always, business as usual.

The table sags under the weight of the world
fallen in fragments on the front page
of yesterday's paper. In Africa, free
of colonial tyranny, a coup d'état,
a change of personnel in a TV show,
the budget overbalances yet again,
boat-people perish in a tidal wave.
You turn, with smugness but good reason, towards
the news that stays news, the Resurrection.
The word is difficult to chew, and lies
heavy on the stomach. It's a question of power
you willingly confess, of wonders waiting
for you to perform them, you whose sins
you've written painfully with an iron pen.
And love, you murmur, don't forget love,
the Father cleaving to the cleft Son,
doubly insoluble, beyond imagining,
more vital than brain, or heart, or breath,
alien to this cold and sentimental fish.
You observe the lonely traffic outside,
huddled and rushed, and time passing
in the form of clouds, a single gull
transmitting the sun on its way to the Seine.
You smile at the rocket of the Ascension, and mean
in deepening shyness to dare the force
that gathers all things together in one.

*

I think I know I feel love for you, Lord
(the signs are few, inconclusive) but
why does such love not, like the tide
of your earth's whole oceans overwhelm me?
I suffer too moderately your inevitable absence.
Wonder is always with me, a life-long friend,
and thankfulness, however slow-paced, and petitions

rise every day like flocks of squeaking starlings, but with love
you have not plentifully endowed your gifted,
autistic child. Which makes
no difference, I know, to what is and will be
required of me. Rain outside,
tapping on the windows,
drumming on the roof of memory, recalls
such reasons for love I am undone
and this (waves of light) that you
love me. Make me
patient and intolerably impatient for your
unavoidable presence.

*

Perverse and righteous oft I strayed,
mistaking the path in the fog of knowledge,
spending my life in naturally preferring
the love of learning to the learning of love.
Give me the height of judgement, Lord,
that teaches one ignorance, and not to judge,
the blessed clarity of vision, of seing
through, and yet sighting the so much more
to be seen. For love, I must go by the way
where there is no way, but only you,
and a fearful openness to every moment.
A priest hurries past with a mobile phone;
hearing confession? Tonight the stars,
not on a black, on a blue ground.

That only day, with its proper weather.
The pristine particulars of it: the hill
dull with habit, the sky crowded
with uncertain menace, the look-alike fields,
not a plane in earshot, all
struck sudden with lightning, different,
disguised, another
landscape, another
state of seeing. What was, what is
that lesser unsunny oneness drained
of earthen colour, but yet
even so, such a clairvoyant
otherworldly paysage, granted
a sheerness of brightness no eye could
recreate? The young man
rooted like a menhir, made
witness to this world awoken, this
glimpse, angry and glad,
blinked, and wondered.

*

The earth climbing slowly under a contour map
of familiar grass to tall ferns and a path,
and then, as I chance to turn, in a far
elsewhere the ordered image of a house,
quietly red. Seen through a gap
in reality, in its own world. The slope
is noisy by comparison. The green bank
and the building in the distance of early Georgian
I remember as a sheer vision, of my
England and more. Within Ham Gate,
the boy who looked aside, and met the cool flame
of a real house, but where? was innocent of knowing
it was Sudbrook Park, the declined club-house,

in Petersham, of a golf club. The waiters tend
this afternoon to shuffle, but the coffee is racy.
The still, rare mansion and the windy rise
returning, stir with idea, and exist
nowhere as such but in the crowded courts
of Memory, muse, and in presence of mind.

*

In grey-flannel shorts, with a long stick
you probe the sweet stream sunken in the earth
inside the familiar, fabulous Gate.
Your small hand (unpicturable, felt as if dreamed)
slips into the cold that quietly absorbs
your arm and you, as your fingers touch
and remember the electric foreignness of a newt.
Watch out for the leech, the monster of these deeps.
The light of childhood is clean, it adds
like the sun nothing but itself to the scene
in a café maybe, a station, a sick-room.
Aux yeux du souvenir que le monde est immense:
wavering green creatures, plants without names,
frogspawn, sticklebacks, the high wall, a whole
ghostly reality, immortal fact.

18

The round table is a little world
where, writing, I live. Silence. There is
below the marble no end of depth.
Sociable words rise from the hoard,
scenes from memory, true or false,
catch the light, quiet ideas
make their way up through the fictive waters.
Its singular body and mind appearing
on the magic paper, the poem opens
to another space, a newer time.
One travels easy in this charmed elsewhere.
Smoke, and peat, from the standing whisky
insinuate my nostrils, a measured hubbub
raises the room and the waltzing waiters.
Paris outside, the light of reality.
On looking up, I remember the strange
poem whose words, in moving, move
to quicken the present moment in this,
a solid and changeable Paris café.

*

A round table and Tigger the only knight.
Nostalgia weeps for innocent selfishness,
for more or less harmless bumptious bounciness.
The rain has stalked off in a huff,
its well-rehearsed number was not applauded.
The new sun illuminates passing girls,
wind plays in their hair, imagination
plays with other parts, lifts their skirts
(in cricket, the leg glance, my favourite stroke),
the Lord's thunderbolt abstains from striking –
it's only words, innocuous fantasy?
There's the uneasiness of growing up:
what earthly use is an earthy mind?
Egoism endangers – the soul? – other people's.

★

Seated thus, with a view to this my
café-table book, I look at Paris and
am drawn to see desk after desk
in each and every study I've made snug
facing the window. A room
is a mind, a window its eyes, or else
a mind is a room, its eyes windows, and where
am I, if not as much
out there as here, in this moveable
nowhere and everywhere forever
with me? A window calls, the world once seen
is summons, a long vocation, you are,
I say to
myself,
what you perceive. I am
nowhere more me than where the light
elects such angles of roof to alight,
the wind gives wings to ghostly leaves,
dead on the pavement otherwise,
and unknown passers-by
pursue and risk their lives.

Are you an English poet, they ask, or a French?
I'm a Russian poet. I always write
in a language I do not know. Myself,
come to think of it, and I
think of it often, am or is
somewhat of a foreigner, alien to all
I'd hoped to be. We are,
says the man without blinking, called to be saints.
I must be
hard of hearing. But do not suppose
joking eases the ache. A mafia boss
is one, a conscious concentrate
of evil, his conscience
sleeping the sleep of the unjust,
snug as a bullet in a chamber.
When the naked sun
floods Sicily with light, he too appears,
dark-suited on the brilliant marble steps,
flanked by his aids. He is himself,
and thinks black thoughts behind black shades.
Poetry is a foreigner's language you are taught
by writing it. And saintliness
a foreign body one exerts oneself
(or not) to assimilate, and become,
learning little – and failing – by little,
line after line of one's life.

★

The poet lives (or does not)
hand to mouth, feeding himself
morsels of word, that munch
quietly, waiting
for Concentration with her flaming wings
to annul the expected and make audible
what is to be said.

Blunt truths are the sharpest
(bite on those two 't's) in law,
religion, politics, and when it comes
to putting coffee in the blood so as to
locate and startle
evasive silence, womb
of language untried, of the tongue
one cannot yet speak, of hollow
rhythmic sound.
Passers-by
wink in the sun. Out of nowhere
intent small birds, unthinking and as if
their life depended on it, ransack an autumn tree
for seeds and creatures.

★

There is no
geography of night, a foreign country
mostly empty, and unchartable.
I cannot help,
listening with Pascal to the eternal silence
of infinite space, however, being
filled with awe. Stars
deep in the sky shed influence, but also
Bodleys of starry-eyed poetry that
burden one's table.
In a world noisy with novels and media
poetry has become, you may have noticed,
almost inaudible. But that
is not the point. Endless silence
of immeasurable dimension is the point,
the mere dot that, by comparison,
makes sensibly unimaginable the incomparable God.
Poetry first of all puts an ear
to this unearthly silence
that speaks before language and its discontent,
and calls a clamorous planet
to quiet and wariness.

(In my head,
borne by glorious transhuman voices,
by 'all the instruments of joy',
a music fearful to hear in its
bitter perfection.)

20

You picture to yourself, in a Burgundy garden,
the apple tree laden that year with store
down to the lawn (a laughing willow),
the grateful branches kissing the ground.
Gourmet and poet, Adam desired
wisely to bite into the pleasant globe
of the apple Earth. In the dead man under
the quick green tree, time is stopped.
Yet bees are busy with the buzz of news
in this the hill country of Judea.
Time stirs in the windy leaves,
gathers and deepens in the quiet trunk.
We know what we do. You picture yourself
lying in the grass to the smell of fruit,
your eyes open to the passing sky,
your mind revolving thoughts of the tree of life.

*

'Something between
a thing and a thought' is what
Samuel Palmer is reported to have said
a painting is. The water touching
the shins of the cows drinks the light,
which varies colour and body in descending
and as you strain, Constable, to see
what light is, in the Stour where it meets
the light in the clouds, and to see afresh
the light and water spreading on the canvas.
Your searching hand is your further eye
that sees as it writes (repeating the light
with such intimate exactness it changes
into itself) a further light, somewhere between
Essex and expectation, our world here and hereafter.
Heroic and patient Constable, you know
what you do. Your absolute

faithfulness changes the light
there on the wall and elsewhere.

*

That portrait in the Louvre, that young,
that youngish man, or maybe
middle-aged, you remember. Those eyes
that look at you, follow you as you
shift your ground. Sitter unknown.
The face expressionless, you'd swear it, yet
so much is expressed, he's calmly happy or
controls his despair. Who? Where?
Regarding his jacket, it regards your surprise,
that alien fabric, that hitherto unseen
play between green and mellower green.
Wherever you look looks back, the dim wall
behind, beneath the shoulder a shadow, or is it
a trick of the dark? The eyes, though merely
painted eyes, as you let yourself
be taken in, defy from another
world? There is
colour, and line, and light, and nothing,
an eye for hands, and wisdom as to how
a soul animates and holds a body
in space and time. Open-mouthed,
uncertain how to look, or what to see,
standing in presence of the canvas you hear
the shushings of the painter's brush.

21

An array of breakwind poplars, busily
minting coins in the breathing air
yields to a havoc of rooks and their
raucous laughter. Meaning? They feed
in the mannerless manner of their cousins on
scraps of poetry, carrion thoughts,
swooping down dark onto the restless
line-scored tragical-pastoral field.
Go back to the beginning. The fowls of the air
how foul are they now? The murderous aerial
rugby of ruffled sleek crows and magpies
in full evening dress shatters the sunlight.

★

'Keel' slices the water without harm and
slides down the Colne whose final washes
varnish the Essex mudflats with purple light.
Gulls shriek in the air like children in playgrounds.
Holding the helm, at one with the wind
revealed in the bellying sail and fanning
my cheek, I know the river's strange
acquiescence, its awesome meekness.
The rudder
shudders with delight. The boat responds
and the river responds, its whole surge
allowing our small craft to work its way.
My hand holds the secret. But, to return
upstream to Wivenhoe, the wind having dropped,
we need machinery. Questioned, the engine
coughs and scoffs interminably before
in sullen silence finally refusing
the customary rhetoric of pulling and coaxing.
We drift, somewhat scared, towards the real
dangers of the North Sea. Roped at last
to a passing buoy, by dint of adjusting

its private parts, the engine splutters
its indignation and chugs into a semblance
of life. We turn, safe, but something is lost.
The relentless outboard allows the river
no chance, and the tiller tells
the current how to submit.

★

Surprised, you see the wind
scurry like a mouse in the rose-bush.
The foliage quivers with delight.
The garden is alive, inhabited.
A presence moves in the grass,
the ash-trees sway in unison,
squadrons of peaceful clouds
resemble time, passing.
And light appears in the backlit
hedge-leaves, and chooses to touch
patches of lawn and wall
and certain high boughs.
It might be a garden painted,
otherwise known and transfigured,
the invisible glimpsed as the magic
eye of the brush proceeds.
Yet the light and the wind are real.
Nothing supernatural occurs.
It's just that by looking you see
the kingdom of heaven is near.

22

The Spanish Main was hot and stormy,
in stories, in half-intelligible films.
(The pleasure of not understanding everything
the mysterious adults said and did)
and of not knowing what a Main was,
or where those jungly shores and smoke-filled seas
were to be found. And the Barbary Coast,
with a different array of coloured costumes
and pirates whose English I silently corrected,
was far from Margate or the Sussex beaches.
And the Levant, teeming with odd
foreigners, and Nutwood where Rupert Bear
met with adventures. Of all these
admit it! the last
is the first to suck or sucker me back
to a childish dream, or an early sign.

*

In the secret bedroom the skinny adolescent
(his legs 'a couple of yards of white tape')
came and went, was there and was not
as folding mirrors on the chest of drawers
flapped their magic wings. To be
or not to be. The boy philosopher's
playing was comic-serious, the self
(all buzzing and hissing) with a saintly grin
gone into the mirror's crack. Despite
all that thinking, am I? Ammaï.
Reading passionately, a life later,
he stumbles on St. Paul's vehemence and rigour
in stating for the benefit of some foolish Celts
that he is and isn't: I am dead, nevertheless
I live, yet not I, there lives in me Another.
An adolescent senior by now, he knows
again that early intermittence of I

– the old thing with flabby flesh that will
insist and the unforeseeable though clamoured-for
quiet comings of the ingratiating Guest –
as eternity looks him sharply in the eye.

★

A delicate green light apparently emanating
from the quiet grass and the orderly trees
illumines the schoolboy, lightly intoxicated
with freedom this midday and intent on exploring
for the first time the further reaches
of a Park by the Thames (on the other side
however, of his thoroughly familiar Jordan).
The trees, progressively more strange and friendly,
guide into the unknown and open suddenly
like a page in a book of tales on a distant
unbelievable palace. He has to hurry
back to school, nursing the dream,
only to discover, at home, on a map,
his vision was the disappointingly explicable
Wren wing of Hampton Court.
The wonder nevertheless did not abandon him,
nor the learning that prodigious places in his mind,
park and palace, led one to another.
In an earlier age Exning had been
a similar window disclosing elsewhere.
The return to Exning (sounds like a title),
to Esselinga in the home of the Angles,
to Gyxeningas and that pleasant way
of naming villages: Gyxa's people,
was not a success. Seen with other eyes
the sad banality of the place dispelled
almost the previous and now precious truth.

23

Here am I, whatever that may mean,
waiting with bated breath to discover
what things, what words, what lines both long and brief
will offer to be caught. (Why no
future tense in English? Its lack
is disturbing, metaphysical.) On nearby tables
other Lipp regulars, islets of being,
cast casual, half-interested glances at the idle
hovering pen and virgin Moleskin.
(Haven't we had an overdose of poems about poetry?
Of the poet entertaining us with himself? Yes)
but the onset, the élan, the where-from of the poem
remain, after all that searching, unknown.
Who writes? And when? In the communion of Saints
one is not one's own. Is one ever? The mind
anticipates
the sound of an idea (the horns of dilemma?),
an unsuspected hoard somewhere of metaphors,
uncharted emotions, present but how?
The white page vibrates, there is nothing more
than natural in its sudden dazzle, the sun
has simply shot through a cloud and touched it.
Yet I'd like the whole café to shake with laughter.
The words
came.
It knows me better than I do, it writes me,
this English language, my mother's tongue.

*

Je n'ai pas oublié, snug at my mother's side,
a child in her bed on Sunday mornings,
singing the hymns she taught me and carols in
and out of season. My father's suits
and shirts hanging on the picture rail. A face
on the walnut wardrobe I took for the devil's

and had, with each furtive glance, pleasure in being scared by.
'All things wise and wonderful.' Why,
Mum, such concern? 'He gave us
eyes to see them, and lips that we might tell.'
You, a stranger to the Bible, apparently
far from the carolling world. Like taking me,
a wondering six-year-old, to Cambridge.
What future, prophetess meek and mild, did you see?
Not your own, violated by cancer and abused
(my God!) by neglect. I have not forgotten
– forgive the rhetoric – your visionary goodness.
I sense you still, showing the way
forward to childhood, calling me to be
a true child wise and guileless;
hoping against hope we shall sing together.

★

Between now and then, in the mean while
the world and myself in Monsieur Lipp's
salon, my Pascal's room, await,
coursing through the heavens though sluggish with it,
the coming catastrophe, a thorough turn,
and final stanza. Who shall I be
among my numerous has-beens and the one
(I have been young, and now am old)
eternally possible? An infant full
of words, I sit here scratching not only
my head and finding my way (though full
also of ignorance) opens of itself.
Life is short, its arse is long,
as the man said, and for friends who've been
an unconscionable time living, the sad flesh
saddens everything. Do not abridge
their aching, Lord, yourself the bridge,
nor mine in the event. As for the new
childhood, hold my heart as I adventure
step by step through days as through a poem,
taking no thought for tomorrow's words.

55

24

The round and laughing soprano rides
the unceasing waves of the sea of Tallis
where whales send their booming voices through huge
deeps and distances. *Excelsis, altissimus,*
  gloria, gloria, gloria, the glory
(what a word! – it's meaning? – in the music –) fills
our ears and belly, all heaven and earth
joyfully noising. And just look at the girl
whose elate, unstoppable song
continues in infinity; and by her side
a tall young woman stooping embarrassed
at being so present yet caught in that sensual
spiritual music; and then a small blonde
swaying oblivious. All dissimilar.
A barrel of a baritone next to a willowy
small-mouthed alto, a quivering beard,
a sergeant barking orders – such
familiar variegation suddenly no longer
obvious. A vision born of the continuous
counterpoint reveals
the contoured thatness of each discrete
creature and, after gripped contemplation,
the concentration of pleasure for God as He makes them
one by one. Miranda's world
that has such people in it. Later,
seen in clairvoyant clarity the fact
(the word has become embarrassing) that He loves
every singularity and them as they are.

*

Some drugs, say those who know, make each
detail focussed on lunge at the eye,
a miracle of itselfness, outstandingly there.
How right they are! Duns Scotus was neither

drugged nor wrong, who observed this sea-stone,
its proper distinction brilliant with its own
life. To name him father of dunces
was in this unjust, unrighteous: he saw
 – or prompts one from a certain distance to see –
in every instance of creation ecceity,
ecstasy. Were he here,
he'd hopefully see the joke, and accept,
for the sake of a higher cause the judgement;
shouldn't a man stand on his dignity
until it deflates? Immortal Duns!
In a world too vivid not to survive
 – too quick to the core – its dissolution
in fire and noise, we are foredoomed
to immortality. Therefore on earth
we must live all ready an immortal life.
Lead me into the holy Saxon
land of uprightness. The word leaps out.

★

'Blessèd' are the peacemakers, not '*heureux*'.
I hear it in the brasserie hubbub, and the word
goes deep. It speaks of a world
still here, seen sideways, differently real.
Am I happy? Yes, as always in
mid-poem, but 'blessèd' is otherwise,
compatible with mourning, torture or common
terminal cancer. A rotten life
upheld day by day by the Spirit is
a generous gift, a work to wonder at.
And 'righteousness' strikes home (how attain it?), whereas
read in a French translation '*justice*'
is bland and general, lacking the body
of sharp particularity. I could probably find
contrary examples to deflate my English
ego, but the voice
quietly loud in my ears is the voice
of Caedmon and Luther, of Mercian hymns.

To hunger and thirst after righteousness is to be
drawn by its eccentric ecceity beyond
justice, understandable virtue, the world.
This morning's coffee, a heady brew,
stands on the window table in the quick of the light.

25

A code and all the walls of Coventry cracked.
And a child covered in rubble-dust reading
graffiti on the smoking stones, and wailing
in the stench and broken teeth of apocalypse.
'After Auschwitz... barbaric.' The parting
bombers offer their steady drone
to whatever Lord's song one may wish to sing.
Churchill in his bunker, the weight of a world
awry on his shoulders, bites the bullet
and the rind of that apple, as the cleaving twins
leap at him. *'In dürftiger Zeit.'*
Remembrance is grievous, the burden intolerable,
in this wide gap of time since the prime
catastrophe occurred, not ending the play
but making it possible. Hitler, the scene
with the mass salute, old-fashioned hubris.
'We hanged our harps', and took them again
many times over. Poetry is after
the break from heaven, the deliberate fault,
the first, savage suicide and murder.
What primitive songcraft can take on
the escapable horror, the poet as everyman
knowing the plague of his own heart, as
a shrewd wind sifts the remains, and during
the fall and shatter of a Dresden figurine?

⋆

The poem's siren song wails in the night
for danger, rising, falling, rising
again and again. We are at war.
Each line a chugging doodlebug (suspense)
waiting for silence. And the light show:
words as searchlights probing the darkness
only so far, crisscrossing like semaphore.
Where is the enemy? Who? Under the gloom

of the song-full trees where an unwise ear mis-
took the sly proposal and from
the end of the earth a cry, defend
us from the gang of our enemies within,
death and our old friend sin. It is all –
gods, heroes, pensive rivers and hills,
love, elegy, the matter of Britain, wit,
memory, numinous objects, dream –
a terrible beauty revealed. It is not
on earth as it is in heaven. That strain,
a level chant now, unhurried, as if
all were clear, all smiles, whereas
the sound contains menace still and will recur.

*

The light glints brilliant on the zinc roofs
in the real painting framed by the window,
and the sky is drenched with blue from the life
of the hidden sun. The unlocking of the eyes
is fruitful and multiplies as language unseals
and words make love to all they name.
The world on my couch. Tell me, tell me
your earliest memory. We children inventing
scrumping, and that taste, delicious and brief.
(The ghosts of wind on the promenade, holidays,
the white and friendly silence of winter.)
Tell me your dreams. Of being new.
With age and looking the glory deepens.
Each line of the poem a trembling threshold
with a view to a stranger world and self
one can only imagine stepping over into.
Yet the posts of the door moved at the voice
hallowing and rapt. The spirit is weak,
the flesh all will. Our cry is Caliban's,
the savage who guides to the coolest springs
and to every fertile inch, and who hears
sweet airs and dreams of the clouds opening.

26

Sweet Thames run softly past my mother's house,
that tiny cottage on your towpath's edge,
where, child and young woman shop-girl she knew
little of anything and acquired wisdom.
In Kew! What business lawyer's or trader's
money possesses it now? The pay
of a corporal had barely sufficed and English
mustard gas killed him. And who remembers
in Richmond Theatre the play you sent
aged 12, or the director visiting and urging
your mother to encourage your gift, whose flush
of shame and indignation at the very thought
of Thespian fleshpots disposed of your desire?
'Cambridge Cottages', as chance would have it
(and chance can be canny), and there I was,
in Cambridge, your hope, in a room above
Milton's (chance can be droll), a writer
with as yet few buds. My clumsy words,
now I am older than you, can they help
allay… compensate… make amends…
fulfil your dream? Sweet Thames, sweet river,
that flowed through my childhood like a thoughtful god,
give power and perseverance to my pen.

*

Of Prince Albert's Royal Laundry the Italianate
tower was landmark, ambiguous lure.
A garage when I knew it, of which, at seventeen,
you were made, Dad, the manager, and a singular house
where Gran and your celibate siblings continued
their strange life. It sounds quite swell,
with views of the Old Deer Park in sought-after Richmond,
but for the smell of petrol and the lonely lockups,
and the cold uncanniness of passages and landing.
You stride in 'Thirties photos by the sea,

smiling, all life before you, already
mortgaged, your father gone, your studies
abandoned, your salary week by week
sustaining your prolific mother's family.
Those highbrow looks, that matchless memory
wasted, you knew, and your son useless,
moving elsewhere, yet, believe me, always
handling your draughtsman's drawings and the exact
wooden rulers that ought to have traced your future.

★

The fog the eyes could walk through seethes
and smothers the boy's head in white darkness.
The long road home is under his feet
but a hidden hand must reach for the wood
of the first garden fence, and then the next,
a single smell in his nose and eerie silence.
An earlier boy, equally my self,
nested in the smallest of gate-leg tables.
A later, alone with his stamps or homework,
opened his ears to another world,
to *Roman Carnival*, *Egmont*, 'what is life
to me without thee?' House by house
he follows his fingers, counting the gates.
And Dad stepping down this same street briskly,
the Daily Chronicle in the crook of his arm,
his broad back humped from desk-work.
And Mum, on the way to the shops, bathed
in the light and scent of an exuberant white
improbable magnolia. A globe of time
or a bubble, while the boy, breathing and almost
becoming fog, inches along.
Mother, father, and the many guises
of your only child: you and I
am one, you are here, history has not
effaced you, now, in this infinite
instant the future rocks. What is
to be done? He touches the familiar gate,
and advances gingerly to the waiting door.

27

Jesus, people, poetry, ideas.
Is Filius Dei, then, the Word
of heaven and earth, one of the balls
I juggle with? In that order at least,
at least in principle. 'And he shall give thee
thy heart's desire.' But what does
the heart desire? Oh do not ask…
The question sends gnawing rats into every
darkness of the sunken self, the answer
being too weighty – wait! – as if my
death depended on it. All those books,
of whose making there will be an end, are treasure
for the heavy heart, so slow to rise
with the alien gravity of love. As for occasional
verse, it must be redeemed, like time,
and Israel, and all your people.

★

Prayer is one thing, quite another is how
throughout the day I appear to you,
a wise man from the west bearing gifts
of guilt, and frank disobedience, and murmur.
So many words, so many ideas:
remain below. Holy learning
(not mine, to become mine) is the way, complexity
of incarnate thought available only
to the simple-hearted, who are and who act
(I see them), in Paris, Cambridge, Kingston,
at the end of the conduit of the upper pool
in the highway of the fuller's field, wherever
the Spirit moves. And learned charity?
To know so as to love, and following your so
practical metaphysics, to learn to save
oneself and others?

To say 'Hallowed be thy name' is like
speaking in tongues. 'Name' has a meaning
deep in some foreign language. 'Hallowed',
echoing with the awestruck gladness of the old
Saxons who invade us still, is still
absorbingly unknowable. Father, keep
aloof, be 'sanctified', effulgent in 'glory';
beyond our grasp yet to windward, whence
the Spirit blows. And rinse our ears
to hear (alone in our secret closet and having
shut the door) the deafening chorus
of creatures out of reach above and below
our dumb selves: heaven alive
with the hailing dead, seas that roar,
mountains shouting, rivers clapping
their hands to acclaim. Admit me to your lore-house,
show me the fields shining with praise,
the sun exalting,
a single tree, itself singing.

28

The stony mass of Turner's watercolour.
The light has scraped rough the intangible masonry
of Old London Bridge, as it streaks and dots
the level Thames with silver and gold.
Gothic windows carved on the piers
return one's gaze. Summary immortal
dabs of humans cross on a horseless carriage.
On a starling below, a large, improbable
standing figure in blue and white,
another in olive green and seated,
startle among the London browns: an Arabian
vision. Arches invite one
through, to eerie buildings rising
from eerier reflections, the sails of a single
windmill, steeples and a second bridge
and further distance. The solidities almost
dissolve, the weighty stonework that looks
other than real might fade and reappear
in ghostly glory, until one finds oneself
perusing a small rectangle of paper.

★

Glenn Gould's stricken arm.
Contrapunctus XIV, like a foreign word
or sovereign, grants one audience. The country,
unknown and nowhere, the bewildering building
moves as one treads with so many feet
the unending and infinitely mobile threshold.
Mathematical avenues crisscross, rebound,
vanish to reappear, in choruses of song
no bird or human has heard nor could reach.
Everything, nothing, is repeated, worlds
turn and return new-lit.
And the mind, discovered, advances with more
organs that it knew, as door after door

opens and closes, as if, this time
or the next, one might step through and beyond.
An upflung arm as the awaited notes
die among the keys.

★

Paris coffee and croissants is the weird
real this morning, and a writing hand.
So high and far beyond the brasserie window
the child-blue sky, innocent of crime,
will dissolve tonight and tomorrow reappear.
Irreplaceable clouds glide through time.
A white gull, giddy with the life
of countless hidden colours of light,
cleaves the invisible. Might not the curtain,
of a blue suddenly uncanny and baffling,
rise, or from heaven to earth be rent?
In a Burgundy garden a glittering sun
enters and unites the air, the old
stones of the walls, the trees standing
as if to attention, the trembling hill.
Lazy buzzards circle above.
Everything stills, slides into eternity,
the scene too real for ordinary summer.
To fall asleep in a world more deeply
being itself in soundless being,
and awake to discover…
The early owl hoots as it passes over.

29

A shower of floating diamonds
glistens in the December sun.
The long road is mantled in ermine.
Tell me, if you know,
the colour of snow?
Observe in the white a fiery red,
orange, and yellow... and tender violet,
and hues reserved for the enjoyment of angels.
Before your eyes, the invisible;
the improbable rainbow.

*

Fish eagles are known to gather there,
over a dark and teeming lake.
We saw them clearly, on the horizon,
and remembered, stepping from the car
into the sharp South African air,
the fame of their wheeling cry.
Full, we had been told, and haunting.
They circled, swooped and slowly rose,
power and grace in our binoculars,
but the wide stillness of the Drakensberg
did not echo with their scattered calls.
Waited for elsewhere we must move on,
leaving the silence to vibrate with sounds
we might have heard.

*

The sea seizes the gaze of the boy
arrested on the cliff-head.
(At Cliftonville, in the land of shades.)
Norway is there, below the horizon,
and Vikings, heaving their ships into the tide.
Death beyond the unfenced edge, and death

in the nauseous wet salt of the irresistible
beautiful, interminable, fish-packed monster.
The North, he wonders; what is the North?
Where they meet, sea and sky vanish.
What other world waits to be discovered
over the hill? And by what eyes?

30

Despite the primitive tackle, at the first
dangling of the line in the water, a bite!
So little, the fish came out onto the bank
with no struggle on its part or the least
effort on mine. On the boy's, that is,
who with friends had crossed to the otherwhere
of the island on Teddington Lock, a country
of peace, and green afternoons in eternity.
Stepping down over onto the familiar ground,
he had mused on the North Sea tide that cruises
through watchful London and is only checked
here at his feet. Downstream was departure,
the Thames and the English hurrying out
to ride the ocean's tiger, the world
all before them. He did not know
innumerable small boats had assembled here
from the length of his silver-blue river to rescue
the Dunkirk stranded. Through disappointment,
he released the fish back down into the current.

★

Him hanging against the sky
he remembered, between two thieves,
intermittently and, writing, recalled
the unfinished vision: 'he was numbered
with the transgressors'. Startled I imagine
Matthew, and exultant, as he repeated
newly the unforgotten find.
Unceasingly the New Testament casts
line after line into its memory, the Old,
leaving nothing unchanged. The act
of memory changes. Memory like
photography is not a realist art,
today's light plays on each recovered scene
as sunlight each day on each day's various faces.

Memory is the name
for the unknown occasional country where among
the looming half-foreign me's the signs
of the real and waiting other-me fitfully glint,
the garden lilac, a Kingston street
appear sometimes, numinous, new-worldy.

★

Seen from the mindful slopes of Montmartre,
from inside a head humming with French
eloquence and bias, England is abroad,
a foreign country, island of faery.
English becomes
a strange tongue echoing readily with names
gainrising with the new-born world they name.
Like poetry heard
anywhere in Albion. The oak in Arden
and Stoneleigh catches the dark in gnarled
recesses cracked with time and without
being the world-tree moves as a giant in the mist.
What more can one say? I shall stroll the Seine,
browse the bookshops, and maybe visit,
one day soon, the Brasserie Lipp.

Notes

Brasserie Lipp: famous literary restaurant-café on the boulevard Saint-Germain in Paris. Almost opposite are the church of Saint-Germain-des-Prés (poems 1 and 8) and the recently baptised place Sartre-Beauvoir (poem 1).

Poem 1   Philaminte: a character in Molière's *Les Femmes savantes*.
Poem 7   Letter of Racine to La Fontaine, 11th November, 1661.
Poem 8   Barbe à papa: candy-floss.
Poem 15   Baudelaire, 'Le Soleil', in *Les Fleurs du Mal*. Boileau, 'Épître VI'.
Poem 19   Purcell, *Come ye Sons of Art*.
Poem 25   'In dürftiger Zeit': '[what use poets] in a time of dearth?' Hölderlin, 'Brot und Wein'.